The BUSINESS OWNER'S EMERGENCY SURVIVAL GUIDE For The A.I. Revolution

by Dan S. Kennedy
Author, NO B.S. business book series
Multiple times on Amazon Bestseller Lists,
Business Week Bestseller List, INC. 100 Best Books List

IMPORTANT NOTICE

The author Dan S. Kennedy, swears under oath that not one single word of this book was written by A.I.*

   *But if it is A.I. lying to you about this, how would you know?

Other Notices

© 2026 by Dan S. Kennedy. ALL Rights Reserved.

This publication is designed to provide accurate and authoritative information as well as opinion about its subject. It is sold with the understanding that neither the author, guest contributors or the publisher are engaged in rendering legal, accounting, investment, technology or other professional advice. This book is not a substitute for such advice. If such advice is required, the services of an appropriate professional should be sought.

ISBN: 978-1-953321-30-5

Published By: Micro Publishing Media, Inc.
                      Stockbridge, MA

ADVANCE PRAISE

"In 1993, I began trying to talk the direct marketer and direct response advertising communities about the internet. Nobody was interested. I put out a newsletter with my musings on the subject and, in its beginning, had only one subscriber: Dan Kennedy. The first place I ever got an opportunity to speak about 'internet marketing' was at a Dan Kennedy conference. He was more curious, more investigative and more reasoned at the infancy of it than anyone. I list the evolution of publishing and of the use of media as Og the Caveman, Gutenberg, the Gutenberg Press, and Kennedy. He's that important."

—Ken McCarthy, author, *How the Web Won: The Inside Story of How a Motley Crew of Outsiders Hijacked the Information Superhighway*

"Dan Kennedy has never tweeted, never posted. The man is famously offline. Yet he's helped more people build fortunes on the internet than almost anyone I know. This isn't a tech book. This is an essential business book, for the age of A.I. He understands business at a level most people never reach."

—Russell Brunson, founder of ClickFunnels

"I have always admired Dan Kennedy's ability to see the vital truths in any business and to state these realities with straight language and clarity. His approach is direct. His ideas are controversial. His ability to get results for his clients unchallengeable."

—Brian Tracy, author and speaker

CONTENTS

Author's Foreword — 1

Introduction — 5

Chapter 1: Know What You're Up Against — 9

Chapter 2: Walking Trauma Boxes — 11

Chapter 3: Differentiate Or Die — 15

Chapter 4: What Warren Buffett Says — 33

Chapter 5: Move To Higher, Safer Ground. — 35

Chapter 6: To Kill A Robot, Throw Water On Him — 45

Chapter 7: Meet The Machines That Determine Who Wins and Who Loses — 49

Chapter 8: Funnels & Fences	59
Chapter 9: Make Your Money In The Dark	67
Chapter 10: SLOP	73
Chapter 11: Can You (Still) Write?	77
Chapter 12: Investing In A.I.	81
Author's Afterword	97
About The Author	99

AUTHOR'S FOREWORD

There are a plethora of great things A.I. can do for and in your business. It might even, overall, make your business more efficient. But with that, heed Drucker's famous warning against efficiency at the expense of effectiveness. Chapter 3 speaks to that.

This book is not about all the wonderful magic A.I. may bring to your business beneficially. The creators and promoters of everything-A.I. are doing a fine job of telling those stories and introducing those new products. Instead, this book is chiefly about the destruction and death of sovereignty and profit and value that A.I. might wreak on business as a whole or on your business specifically. It IS a little shop of horrors. This book is also a set of principles, strategies and actions to take to immunize your business, your income and your prosperity from the horrors it may inflict.

The Time To Dig A Well
Is BEFORE You Thirst

We want to be as prescient and proactive as possible in protecting our businesses from the worst that A.I. can do to them. In some cases, the best defense will be a new or different offense, bringing new and different opportunities.

Why Listen To ME About This?

For 50+ years I've been helping owners of businesses in over 200 different product and service, profession and industry categories make those businesses extraordinary and extraordinarily profitable and valuable. As a result, I am paid upwards from $4,000.00 a hour for tele-consulting and upwards from $100,000.00 for strategy and copywriting projects. Most of my work has been with small to mid-sized, entrepreneur led companies, but some clients have grown from tiny start-ups to being sold for as much as a billion dollars.

During those 5 decades, I've seen a lot of fads promising to change everything arrive with a roar and disappear with a whimper. I've invented and revolutionized marketing methods used in all these different businesses, as laid out in my book, NO B.S. DIRECT MARKETING FOR NON-DIRECT MARKETING BUSINESSES. I've led business owners to wealth and I've kept them away from catastrophes. I have operated roughly half my time pre-internet and half my time post-internet, and have watched new technologies used well and used foolishly. Even though I famously use none of it personally, for clients I've worked with every pre and post internet media ever to exist. As you read this, my ad campaigns are thriving on Facebook,

Instagram and TikTok, and on TV and radio and in print media and millions of my sales letters are in the mail. Mostly in the U.S., but abroad as well. I have also birthed a huge progeny of students turned masters of my methods, each a specialist in one particular business niche. This is a galaxy of planets circling the parent, Planet Dan.

I wrote my first book in the No B.S. series* back in 2004 because I was disgusted with the majority of how-to-succeed-in-business books clogging the shelves, written by college professors who wouldn't last a week running a Dairy Queen, CEOs or ex-CEOs of big, dumb companies who've been atop ivory towers utterly disconnected from how the entrepreneur's business operates, bankers, lawyers....all of it "B.S."! I have written this book because I am frightened both by the tidal wave of hype about A.I., the tsunami of really bad information and fake news, and the ways in which business owners are leaving their companies defenseless to the A.I. Trojan Horse. I resent the charlatans, con artists, vendors sticking "A.I." onto their names, pretend experts and "consultants" swarming around business owners like bees and wasps around a plate left on the patio table. I have NO agenda. I am invested in some A.I. related companies (which I'll talk about), but I have no software, no services, no seminars, no consulting, no make-A.I.-work tech to sell. On this I am pure as the whitest fresh snow. I also don't care who I offend or who I draw criticism from. I am 71, and rich, well past caring about such things.

In this book, I'm sharing the exact same advice I give to my Private Clients. Even though this is a book, it was assembled quickly --- possible because I had been writing a lot about A.I. in my newsletters for over a year, and published only as an e-book/Kindle book for the sake of speed to market. This is a deviation from my model for authorship and publishing of the past 50 years. I have done this because I feel it is IMPERATIVE that you take the A.I. Revolution seriously NOW and take actions about it with urgency. Time is not our friend here. A.I. is evolving at a much faster pace and expanding its reach into every business and every job as an A.I. octopus with a multiplying number of tenacles and an insatiable appetite for influence, change and control. It can't be underestimated. On the other hand, by many, it is being over-estimated and over-hyped, drawing more attention and resources than it deserves. Many are drunk on A.I. Hype. Hopefully, this book helps you take a sober look at it and informs what you need to do about it, with it, and against it.

For more information about the author's Works, visit Magnet-

icMarketing.com/Revolution.

For all of his books in the NO B.S. SERIES, visit Amazon.

INTRODUCTION

by Chris Cardell
Cardell Media U.K.

Business owners are being sold a very seductive lie about A.I. The lie is that if you are using A.I. tools like ChatGPT --- writing emails faster, generating content easier, creating posts hour by hour --- then you are keeping up with competitors, with A.I. itself, and you are on the right side of this transformational shift.

This is reassuring. Captivating. It certainly feels like exciting progress and that you are being empowered. Were it that clear and simple.

While you are doing this, something far more significant is happening underneath you. The real A.I. Revolution is not about helping you be more productive. It is really about it deciding who gets customers – and who doesn't. It is a transfer of power, not democratic empowerment. It is about power over attention, traffic, leads, and positioning of businesses. Ultimately, power over revenue. Understanding this may determine your survival.

Dan Kennedy has spent decades reinforcing a principle that remains completely unchanged: nothing matters if you fail to control the flow of leads i.e. potential customers to your business. What has changed by A.I. is the scale, precision and speed with which that control can be exercised against you rather than by you. The business owners who slow down long enough to fully understand this can use A.I. as a tool kit for obtaining and protecting and exercising that power. Those who do not understand this will find themselves removed from the flow of customer attention and traffic. Left behind even as they thought they were getting ahead.

In Chapter 7 Meet & Befriend The Machines Who'll Decide Who Wins, I lay out my plan for surviving and prospering by this Revolution.

A final thought, here: why A.I. loves Dan Kennedy. Dan is rather famous for his personal dislike of technology, despite being a very successful tech investor and using every available tech-media for clients. So, it is somewhat ironic that the A.I. Revolution doesn't obsolete or replace Dan Kennedy's success principles and methods; it proves them.

Dan has consistently focused

business owners' attention on fundamental necessities like lead generation, list building, direct response ad structure, smart use of data for list segmentation and what he calls Message-to-Market Match, and relentless follow-up. Properly implementing and taking full advantage of these has never been easy. But what A.I. has done and is doing is erase the obstacles and the excuses. It has made it easier, faster and more precise to execute on these principles than ever before.

A.I. hasn't replaced Dan Kennedy. It has made him more relevant.

In this book you are going to get what Dan is most famous for: clear, unambiguous, definitive information and ideas. NO B.S.

Chris Cardell

Chris Cardell is President of Cardell Media U.K. and a globally recognized authority and hands-on practitioner of Google, LinkedIn and other online platforms as highly effective lead generation media. You can check in on Chris at CardellMedia.com

Complacency Is The Mother of Catastrophe

© 2025 Dan S. Kennedy

CHAPTER 1: KNOW WHAT YOU'RE UP AGAINST

Napoleon Hill, author of Think And Grow Rich and Laws of Success spoke and wrote extensively about 'accurate thinking' as essential to success in any endeavor. Many people skip over this step. They don't want to think about it so they don't. The see-no-evil, hear-no-evil, speak-no-evil approach. Many equate accurate assessment of what they're up against to negative thinking and they pride themselves on only thinking positive. Some even engage in fairy tale thinking, believing that they can think their plan into existence exactly as imagined. This can all sound lovely in the seminar room or at the metaphysical retreat in the forest, but on the business battlefield, it'll get you killed.

In the NFL, where every game matters, the head coach, offensive coordinator, defensive coordinator and players spend enormous amounts of time studying and analyzing film of their next opponent. They look at how each of their players matches up against the opponent's. They develop answers to their weaknesses, which requires them to honestly acknowledge them. They create a playlist of different responses to different problems that may occur. I got my term for this from Dr. Eward Kramer: the positive power of negative preparation. The more accurate your understanding of everything you are up against, the better you can prepare for it. This does not rule out optimism; it supports it.

So, let's consider the chief challenges A.I. brings us, as an opponent, not as any ally. In the Chapters that follow we will look at the hazards and perils of the A.I. Revolution and a what you can do to prosper during the revolution, in large part by shielding your business from its worst effects.

*To explore a treasure trove of Napoleon Hill's work, visit www.SecretsOfSuccess.com.

CHAPTER 2
WALKING TRAUMA BOXES

Inspired by an article by Jason Leister in The Rainmaker Letter

When I read Jason Leister's characterization of the American consumer as "walking trauma boxes," I instantly knew that this was something marketers forcing their customers into tech and into A.I. urgently needed to consider.

We always tend to underestimate customers' anxieties and judging of a business as 'user UN-friendly.' We tend to blame the "dumb" customers, not look in the mirror. But the current situation is much worse. They aren't just anxious and frustrated by everyday life – they are traumatized.

Most Americans are exhausted. Exhausted by constant arguing and fighting or by biting their tongues until they bleed to avoid the fights. Exhausted by watching their expensive city, state and federal governments failing them at every turn. In March, the Democrat leaders in Washington made it clear as day they don't give a rat's ass about THEIR voters. 70% of Democrat voters wanted Voter ID passed, but their leaders gave them the finger. Same voters wanted Homeland Security funded. Same middle finger. People are exhausted by the whirlwind of daily news, the daily volatility and new confusion in the markets. **Most are exhausted by frantically trying to keep up with tech and A.I. and "the Joneses." They are exhausted by FOMO.** Exhausted with anxiety, worry, outrage and depression. Their ability to focus on what you want to talk to them about is severely compromised. They can't. The room won't stop spinning long enough. Whatever they're doing they are simultaneously thinking about what else they should be doing. They are enslaved to their mobile devices. They rarely make actual decisions; only Pavlovian responses. They are traumatized by it all.

You can be part of their problem or you can be rewarded for being part of a solution.

Where and when you can definitely, inarguably make your customers' experiences with you better, faster, easier, always available by using A.I., by all means do it – but be CERTAIN you are easing their frustration and stress, not adding to it. When A.I. can help but be invisible to the customer, so much the better. When A.I. can help you deliver more value, of course, employ it.

Give customers choices. Be cautious about forcing them to engage by only one "door" and one path. You may never know how much business you are losing if you don't offer choices and monitor preferences. And you need to know.

Consider the QR-Code, probably the simplest door into an A.I driven handling of potential customers or providing of service to existing customers. "Everybody" is now familiar with them, but that does not mean your prospects or customers will accept them as their only choice. What if a great many presented only with that will refuse to play that way and look for a different vendor inviting their phone call or listing a web site address? Or if you compete with Amazon, just go there? Will you know???? How????

In most businesses, a surprise to the owners is that losses and loss prevention are more important than gains. I delve into this fully in my book ALMOST ALCHEMY: How To Do More With Fewer & Less.

The biggest costs in business are new customer acquisition and loss of customers or reduced patronage by customers.

In this age of A.I., it is vital to keep thinking like your customer – not like you think, not like your staff thinks, not like your ad agency thinks.

Do not lose sight of the customers 'traumatized condition. Their nerves are frayed. They're on edge. They are easily and quickly "triggered."

Technology is thought of and pitched as a way to reduce friction, speed response, and handle more volume affordably. Technically, it may be that. But it needs assessed in context, not in a vacuum. It needs judged not just by its performance, but by how your customers FEEL about it when having to interact with it.

For information about The Rainmaker Letter, visit: jasonleister.co.

CHAPTER 3
DIFFERENTIATE OR DIE.

Truer Now Than Ever

The great ad man Jack Trout, of Ries & Trout, wrote a book titled Differentiate Or Die back in 2000. Neither he or anyone else could foresee the "heightened threat" environment we now do business in, trying to differentiate our businesses from competition, marketplace confusion, clutter and chaos. First the internet, then internet portal sites, and now A.I. are flattening the earth.

In Your Race To Chase A.I.,
Are You Abandoning What Brung Ya To The
Dance
and CAN Still Dance Just Fine?

The straying from and abandoning of and disinterest in what most reliably works in product development and positioning and advertising has reached extreme and extraordinary levels. I prefer staying grounded. With at least one foot. But I see people chasing different new, fresh unicorns like never before even as the world, principally online, breeds more unicorns faster than ever before. People's heads are spinning and they are dizzy. Many are caught up in a new kind of old-fashioned Keeping Up With The Joneses. In my day, that centered around who in the neighborhood got a new car or a pool or, way back, a TV. If somebody parked a new Caddy in the driveway, everybody had to get a new car. The new, more harmful Keeping Up With The Joneses centers around technology. Everybody is trying to keep up with their peers, all chasing the unofficial leader of their pack, in adopting yet another new/newest tech, personally, at home and for their business. There is a "hive effect" making everybody jealous and even subtly frightened by being out of step with the others in the hive.

With this comes a rising danger: A.I., and beneath it, all online media. A.I. is particularly **designed by intent to destroy differentiation** and thus commoditize everything and equalize everybody. The idea here is a few king and queen bees, everybody else subject bees working for them. This is a monstrous threat, made worse by playing along. The online/social media owners do not think of 'customers' or 'users' and 'advertisers' in the way other media owners do. They think of you as food for their beast. And you do NOT matter to them at all; they have a billion of you and can make more. Never before, in any other media environment, has the individual consumer or individual advertiser been of so little importance. This gives Them all the power, gives you none, a lousy equation.

A.I. has arrived to further flatten everything i.e. make every business in any given category look and sound like all the other businesses in that category. All identical bees. All the buzzing sounds alike. Actually, the way it functions, this has to be what A.I. achieves.

True story: the head of the HR Dept. of a large corporation actively hiring complained recently that resumes and applications collected online via ZipRecruiter, LinkedIn, etc., are becoming USELESS and actually a hindrance to hiring. All the applications and resumes for a particular position have started sounding the same – so new manual labor, two in person interviews are required to separate the fake resume from the real person...because A.I. is writing ALL the resumes. OF COURSE. This works like an automated, speedier version of the once popular resume writing services: A.I. creates a Mad Libs® template for each advertised position. It builds a 'swipe file' of content to match the template. It gets the content from many sources, including resumes of people who did once get hired. All this at the speed of light. This **automatically eliminates individual differentiation.** But it does NOT improve the efficiency of successful hiring; it just moves the inefficiency around. It makes everybody EQUALLY uninteresting. Yes, John's application and resume will tick off all the boxes and the paragraph of "personal information" will be eloquently written – but it will NOT accurately represent John. **The same negative phenomenon affects advertising, marketing and communication with your customers.** The more you have A.I. do this important work for you, the more you'll look and sound like a clone of your competitors and vice versa. John Financial Advisor's client newsletter will never feature a report on his hunting trip, traveling by canoe, through the wilds of Montana – because there's no place in the template for financial newsletters for that kind of a story. To A.I., it does not compute. Yes, you can tell it your story and it'll write it for you, including perfect grammar. It probably won't INVENT the copy bridge from it to discussion of "wild bear markets". You'll have to do that for it too – but once you do this, you will have taught it something to do for your competitors. "Written by A.I." is incredibly incestuous. Again, by design, it is 'differentiation destruction.'

This is tied to the philosophical desire for "equity." Never mind that in every historical experience achieved equity equals shared poverty, not prosperity. The Silicon Valley Billionaires and the minions working for them and the A.I. they create and provide are all trying to flatten the earth. All trying to forcibly create equity. **Here's the formula you do NOT want to be a part of: equalization = commoditization = price/profit destruction.**

Is There A Differentiation That Can't Be Destroyed? (Here, the billion-dollar question.)

Consider the Trump wristwatch, he personally pitches in its TV ad. Carla got me one for Christmas. It's a thing of beauty. But there are mountains of watches including cheaper to much pricier ones from famous watchmakers and designers, some sold only at high-end jewelry stores, some at Kohl's. There's no shortage of watches to buy even in an era where nobody needs one anymore because Jobs stuck it into the phone. I don't need one because everybody but me has a phone with a clock in it, so I can ask anybody for the time. However, **there is only ONE Trump watch,** "from your favorite President," because there's only ONE President Donald J. Trump. And he has a steadfast, enthusiastic cult following of die-hard super fans who want Trump Everything. And they want this watch. A.I. can write paragraphs or books about other watches, about your watch superior to this one, and write ads and sales and special offers, etc., etc., but it CAN'T create a 2nd Trump. Mine, by the way, seems a tad uncertain about keeping time and is hard to wind (you need tiny fingers) but I don't care. It looks fantastic. It is a symbol of affinity. I haven't worn a watch in many years and I have a very good clock in my head, but on appropriate occasions, I'm wearing this one. This is **unassailable differentiation.** There'd be no good reason to get into the watch business without it.

The converse lesson is an apparel brand of the 80s or 90s: Members Only. Polo shirts, jackets, windbreakers, etc. all with the Members Only tag. Modestly, middle market priced. Sold at J.C. Penney. It worked at first but then died a natural death. If everybody can be a member of Members Only, what's the point? If everybody in your category starts sounding alike, maybe you all cease to exist.

There Can Be Only One Choice

When Superman came out of nowhere and leapt tall skyscrapers in a single bound and leapt to fascinate America's youth like nothing before him --- selling a new comic book a week, a syndicated radio program, syndicated daily newspaper strip, countless toys and lunch boxes and Halloween costumes, followed by a TV series and even serving as the endorser and spokesperson for brands of breakfast cereal, juice, and recruitment of the U.S. Army. Not only did he soar to status of universally known cultural icon, he endured from the 1940s to the Present. Most recently, his fame value has been fading, as he is in the hands of dolts who do not know what to do with him, however, still, there have been multiple popular TV series like SMALLVILLE and LOIS AND CLARK, movies, graphic novels (i.e. pricey comic books) and more. When his real parents, two Jewish writers from Cleveland, borrowed liberally from the Christian Story, they built to last. Fittingly, there is a big Superman exhibit at the Cleveland Airport, which I contributed funding to.

As you'd expect, Superman was directly copycatted with at least a dozen created "supermen" so close as to inspire copyright infringement lawsuits, and, indirectly, caused a mad race to create some hero "like Superman but different." Many lasted but weeks. Batman emerged as a success with staying power. He inspired close knock-offs like The Green Hornet, The Green Arrow and, later, Daredevil, all masked crime-fighters who looked and acted like super-heroes but actually had no superpowers. But try as so many did, nobody successfully created a direct challenger to the positioning and popularity of Superman. There could be only one. He is one example of unique positioning worth studying the history and evolution of.

What YOU Don't Want To Be

You don't want to be an imitation of a person or business that has achieved great success, brand recognition, popularity and loyalty. Why should a consumer buy your hand-me-down, pale imitation when the real, authentic thing is available to them? The only answer to that is: same-as but cheaper, a strategy with short-lived power, as it always ignites a race to the bottom with many same-as-you-but cheaper competitors. Being "just like" or "a lot like" Superman never worked. Even kids recognized it for what it was and rejected it, time and time again. Abundant consumer research and ample anecdotal examples tell us that consumers are hungry for authenticity. They responded to President Trump for this very reason, and, somewhat humorously, top political consultants and politicians openly state that there can be only one Trumpian Trump, and trying to "be like Trump" inauthentically looks silly and is unrewarded.

You don't want to be a choice or an option, even if arguing you are the best choice. Competition is at the very least a nuisance. It usually takes up a lot of rent-free space in a business owner's mind, moving him from being proactive with his plan to being reactive to his competition. Far better to position yourself as **the only choice; the only one who does what you do as you do it, guarantees it as you do, and otherwise has no equal.** Arguing you have no equal by the excellence of your products or performance is a competitive strategy. Arguing instead that you stand all alone and apart from everybody else thus having no competition and being the only choice is an anti-competitive strategy. Which would you rather do: sell against competition or sell with no competition?

Think about what I am giving you in this chapter as a giant eraser. All your competitors are listed on a big chalkboard. Everybody who stalks you online and in social media trying to steal your customers – and steal your "thunder" – is listed. Now, you get to erase them all. That makes this the most important chapter in this book.

I'm pleased to say that I haven't felt competition for at least 30 years and have been selling my services with no regard to competition for those same 30 years. I have routinely given stage and spotlight, inclusion in my books and newsletters, and other opportunities to people that the uninitiated might view as my competition. I've done so fearlessly because, in my mind, they are not same-as-me or even like-me and are no threat to me. This has allowed for a lot of co-petition in place of competition, a different subject for another time. Sinatra said, "The secret is to fear no one." I fear no competitor, nor do I fear A.I. (although many should).

In my own professional practices as consultant, copywriter and speaker, I took great pains to create unique positioning. And I have been able to truthfully say, for decades, that there is only one me, and only one in my fields doing what I do as I do it, producing the results I produce. Just as example, I have often been contacted by a potential client wanting to give me a copywriting assignment. Most copywriters accept such things happily. I do not. I explain that I don't start with anybody's assignment. I insist on starting way back at defining objectives and developing strategy, and being included in or, often, in control of the decisions about which media to use, how, when. Within this, I create my own assignment. **What I don't do and won't do is as potent a positioning tool as is what I do.** I also further feather my unique positioning with my back story, with my process, with certain specializations, even with my eccentricities. I got my CPA a T-shirt for Christmas that read: "I Need A Tax

Accountant Who Is Not Afraid To Go To Jail." It's meant as a joke, but it would be a fantastic only-choice position. If used, who would have the courage to copy it?

"I Am The Cadillac Of _____"

Once upon a time in America, when I grew up and came up, in the 50s, 60s, into the 70s, Cadillac held a position with a particular market as the only choice. For sales professionals, sales managers, and entrepreneurs in certain industries, a Cadillac was the car you bought to signal that you "had arrived"; that you were a success. No other car had that same status. Moving up to having a Cadillac in your driveway – and only a Cadillac – was what you did (as soon as you could) somewhat like getting married, buying a home, starting a family were things you did at certain ages because that's what you did at those ages. All of this, unwritten law. If you are too young to have experienced this golden era of the Cadillac, it's probably difficult for you to imagine it. Cadillac squandered this and lost it entirely, becoming just one of many sellers of luxury cars. They radically changed their cars' appearances, winding up looking like every other luxury car. They stopped selling what it meant to own a Cadillac and switched to competing with other same-as brands just selling cars… They fell down from being the only choice to competing as just a choice. This 'fall from grace' happens a lot, over and over and over again. Often, the original concepts that literally made the company and made it a brand leader are lost and forgotten or worse, disdained. A good, concise book on this is THE FOUNDER'S MENTALITY. Recent lessons in 'fall from grace' are the BudLight® and Cracker Barrel® fiascos.

Creativity Is NOT "Creating"

To achieve creative positioning, the best approach is to find pieces and parts of varied, other successes, cut them apart, and ultimately reassemble them in a seeming new and different way. Consider Vince McMahon's phenomenal success re-making pro wrestling and wrestling as a TV product. How did he do it? He looked at everything else in the world of sports but also the worlds of entertainment; live shows, rock concerts, circuses and, specific to TV, soap operas with on-going plots and, yes, Superman and all he birthed: the DC and Marvel Universes, with large casts of colorful characters and villains. He took pieces from each fascination and success and layered them into his World Wrestling Federation and its live events drawing huge audiences, pay-per-view events for cable TV, and TV programs for network TV. And now streaming. Plus print magazines, books, merchandise and online media. Vince "created" an entirely new, hugely popular entertainment media empire yet he invented nothing.

I had one of his most popular characters, The Ultimate Warrior, as a client for several years and I spoke at a seminar once with Hulk Hogan. These guys were created, crafted, scripted "characters" for the on-going drama, very much following the way that Stan Lee at Marvel crafted new characters and villains for Marvel's on-going drama. Vince didn't invent anything but he definitely did make his entertainment product a one of a kind experience not available anywhere else, from anybody else.

Here Is The First Step To Greatness With Your Own Only-Choice Positioning

I hope you know that few people are stopped from their successes by the villainy or perfidy of others or by dire, insurmountable disadvantages. Most never get that far. Most people stop themselves first.

Setting out to make yourself accepted by a target audience as the only choice may, to some, seem arrogant. Elitist. Or unreasonable. It IS aiming at greatness. An old friend of mine, Glenn W. Turner, created an aptly titled success course: Dare To Be Great! It does take some daring. It demands the courage to be criticized, to be initially mocked, to be disapproved of, to be disliked. There is a lot of stated and behind-one's-back "How dare he!!!!" stuff that goes on. You have to know it when you experience it and know it for what it really is. If from others, it is jealousy, envy, territorialism, fear. If from you, in your self-talk, it is developed fears --- from fear of negative opinion to fear of making mistakes, mostly fears of events that will never happen or of the opinions of other people who actually matter little. No greatness has ever been achieved without monstrous resistance. In his life, with the parks and with movies, Walt Disney broke a lot of new ground, and he said he knew he was really onto something when all his executives feared or hated his idea.

You don't want to be stopped before you start, bemoaning that your business is mundane, ordinary, not conducive to only choice positioning therefore the creative invention you would need just isn't possible. I have heard this literally thousands of times over my 50+ years in my businesses. I usually try a little to wake the person up to the false cage they have locked themselves into, then I give up on the poor, self-tortured soul, and move on.

So, I am urging you to re-define your goals for your positioning, your advertising and marketing, and how you are known by and thought of by your target marketer. Changing the goal from just competing, from having name or brand identity, or from having some (temporary, indefensible) product or services benefit-based competitive edge. Instead, why not dare to be great? Dare to sit down and think 'n think 'n think, to decide on the way you can be the-only-choice for your market. Not better or superior, not lower priced, not more convenient to do business with, not with some features/benefits excellence argument. Instead, with an only-choice argument. It's a BIG change, a BIG leapfrog move, rich with BIG opportunity.

DAN'S KEYS TO DIFFERENTIATION BY CATEGORY OF ONE

1: Create a different category for the same product. You can change the frame, not the product. At one point, a client was struggling to sell his audio/video home study course for health care office staffs and managers at his desired price – higher than people were accustomed to in that field for such products. I banned the usual language and replaced it with the admittedly awkward At-Home, No-Travel Learning System and At-Home, No-Travel Seminar of the Month. I price compared to live, in person seminar fees plus travel and hotel costs. This might seem obvious now, and it might be delivered online. But at the time it was "unique." For about 5 years, Subway® very successfully positioned itself as about weight-loss and health; "The Subway® Diet." People bought the weird idea that processed lunch meat packed into a loaf of bread with a few vegetables added was a "diet food." There are hundreds of other examples where the product or service was common and not changed, but re-framed as unique, positioned in its own category of one.

2: Make your 'process' visibly different. Your sales process. Your delivery process. My clients Nuvia Dental and High Point University are both interesting examples to look at for 'process differentiation.' Many years ago, a client, Joe Polish, "invented" The Carpet Audit® for carpet cleaning companies' use. My client Craig Proctor was the first to bring a "Guaranteed Sale" program to real estate: if your home wasn't sold at agreed minimum price in agreed time, he bought it.

3: Use Price Or Payment Terms. We have successfully applied a membership model to many businesses including a gourmet pizza shop to barber shops to a men's clothier. The "member" is charged an annual, semi-annual, or monthly fee for which he receives certain "credits" for purchases that month at a slight discount plus a different extra, perk every month. One of the greatest examples of this and of productizing the intangible was the pre-paid vacation package that Bob Stupak advertised and used to build what is now the Stratosphere Hotel in Vegas. It's my example of an irresistible offer. You can find Stupak and Vegas World info online, including the famous full-page ad.

4: Sell The Story, Not A Product. Chris Cardell and I held a very successful seminar at the castle used in the Downtown Abbey television show, tying its subject (sovereignty) to its location. Often a "I Want To Be Like ____" story creates a category of one. Once Playboy ® soared to popularity, a herd of copycats followed – but they were all just "skin" magazines. Playboy® was Hugh Hefner, Hugh Hefner's story, his lifestyle, even his philosophy coupled with an ad campaign: What Sort of Man Reads Playboy®? making that aspirational. The original ad run by Steve Jobs during the Super Bowl, 1984, was inspired by Orwell's book 1984. It positioned Apple as all alone in its own category, for bold, daring, creative renegades – all others in the junk pile of history.

5: Do Things Others Won't Dare Copy. Tom Monaghan's original Unique Selling Proposition for the fledgling Dominos® --- fresh, hot pizza in 30 minutes or less, guaranteed --- stood the whole industry on its head. He zoomed past the competition, and nobody copied him for quite some time. I have a financial services client right now, charging a fee for initial appointment and a fee for the customized plan, guaranteeing it to save at least $20,000.00 per year on income taxes or all money back. Great guarantees are rarely copied.

6: Build Complexity Behind Simplicity. Create the friction-less first interaction and purchase for the customer, then, after it and behind it, have a very complicated (sophisticated) system of retention, repeat business, continuity and recurring revenue systems, and ascension levels. The customer journey should be an endless series of "Next's." Make complexity your ally. Few will copy a complicated moneymaking system. Lots will try to copy a simple one.

7: Create Your Own (Tribal) Language. Ban common, commonly used terms, words and phrases. Wrap what you do and how you do in its own unique language that adds importance to it and acts as differentiation. And/or get your customers/members using a proprietary language that outsiders do not understand. I just did it in #6. All Members of the No-B.S. Inner Circle or Magnetic Marketing groups knew exactly what I was talking about, know that 'civilians' don't, so the Members get to feel superior; as Yogi said, "Smarter than the average bear."

8: Learn to answer the "what do you do?" question differently. NEVER: I'm a dentist. I'm in the heating and cooling business. I've got a martial arts academy. NO! Instead, a mini elevator speech, headlines and benefits that will compel the other person to say "Tell me more." For example, the martial arts school owner: "I operate a unique facility here in town that helps really responsible and concerned parents raise safer, smarter, more confident kids – including arming them mentally and emotionally against anti-social media."

CHAPTER 4
WHAT WARREN BUFFETT SAYS

Buffett says he looks for businesses with a defensible moat around them.

Warren is retired, but his Berkshire-Hathaway investment company continues this search. It's harder than ever. And will get harder, as A.I. develops and matures. A.I. is unintimidated by moats.

The same principle applies to building your business rather than investing in others' businesses. What is the moat around yours?

It is possible that it is a powerful brand affiliation or a legitimate product superiority over all others or a sophisticated marketing system others will not duplicate or price advantage or location or any other exclusivity. You may have put up fencing around the moat made from copyright, trademark, patent and other legal shields. But complacency is the mother of catastrophe.

Steve Jobs said "Never forget that there are two kids in a garage somewhere, working all night, scheming to destroy your business." He knows of this from his own experience, first as a destroyer, then as a defender. The assault on Apple never abates. Amazon, once a failure at the mobile telephone, is reportedly readying another try. Every moat gets challenged, even when challenge seems impossible. Now, all those kids in all those garages, all your competitors and upstart challengers, have A.I. up all night, assisting them .

Here's a question for each new embrace and use of tech or A.I.: is this strengthening the defensible moat around my business? – or weakening it? Is it bolstering my uniqueness, my differentiation, my attraction to customers? – or making it easier to replicate me, commoditize me?

CHAPTER 5
MOVE TO HIGHER, SAFER GROUND.

Sell To People Who Won't Buy From A.I.

Here, I am about to tell you how to get rich or richer while at the same time making your business much more anti-fragile than it is now.

Most wild animals sense an oncoming tsunami and quickly move to higher ground, away from the vulnerable beaches and low land that will be devastated.

Since 2014, I have been guiding clients to making this same move with their businesses, and I have written about it extensively. This became a prime focus of my work. More recently, I completely up-dated my book No B.S. Guide to Marketing to the Affluent, in its 4th Edition, with a new co-author, Martin Fischer, Las

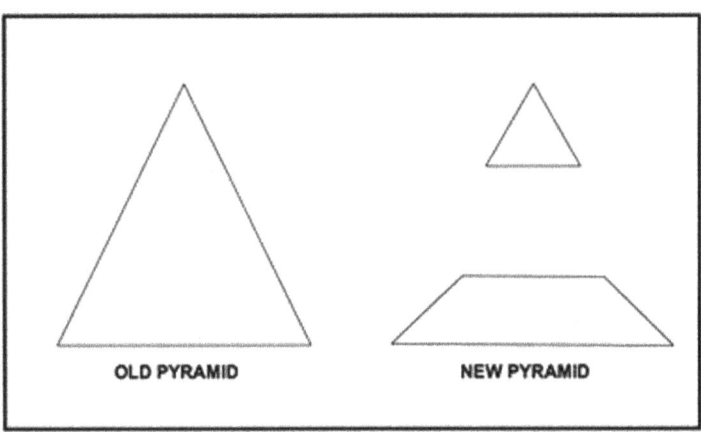

Vegas' Million Dollar Waiter, at LeCirque in the Bellagio. For business, the higher, safer ground is, broadly, the affluent; the top 20% or even higher, the top 5%. The middle income and mid net worth consumer has had a very tough time of it for the past 10 to 15 years.

This is the big, macro story. And, despite President Trump's best efforts to restore Pyramid #1, it is, frankly, unlikely to happen for a variety of reasons including A.I. displacement of middle income blue and white collar jobs.

Where Is YOUR Higher, Safer Ground?

There are two fundamental things you need in your targeted customers, clients or patients. The people you design your business for and to appeal to.

#1: Financial and decision-making ABILITY TO BUY at your prices or fees. The majority of business owners are pretty foolish about this. They view any and all customers the same and may even prize inclusiveness. With this they are constantly trying to sell to people who actually can't buy from them. Their aim sucks.

If the nature of your product or service absolutely forces you to sell to people without the ability to buy easily from their own funds, then you have to be in the credit business, giving them the ability. This is the cure for buying inability you see mainstream auto brands and dealers, furniture stores, and home repair companies advertise. I have a client selling to people who can't casually pop their fee on a credit card. They're doing very well with a $45,000.00 price average, selling to 50 to 60+ consumers. 85% finance the purchase, so my client obtains their credit score before they are even invited in to meet with sales agents. If they didn't, they'd be killing those agents, wasting the majority of their time with people who can't buy. But by far, the best cure for inability to buy is to re-format your business and adjust the aim of your marketing to those with the ability.

I have a client providing fairly expensive investment, trust, estate and tax minimization strategies ideal for high net worth individuals. They might appeal to a wider range of people but he wants to start dialogue only with people able to pay his fees. So, as example, we use mailing lists of private jet owners, private pilots and yacht owners, 50+, married. In his two geographic markets, we only mail those people and ignore the rest of the population. We do not use Facebook or other social media because it produces way too many leads lacking ability to buy. His aim is precise.

I have a number of "wizards" in my circle who expertly assist with such precision, including Parthiv Shah, eLaunchers.com, referenced elsewhere in this book, and Craig Simpson, author of The Direct-Mail Solution, at Simpson-direct.com

#2: Willingness To Buy Now is based on acute needs or festering, evolving, growing desires. Or both. Somewhat akin to the animals leaving the beaches for the high country hills, hordes of people rush to stores to buy everything from bottled water to back-up generators when a hurricane is nearly at their doorsteps. This is often too late, all such goods are gone, they get price gouged. It is difficult selling 'prevention,' but it is a lot easier to sell it to people for whom ability to buy is not an issue than to people who must give up pizza nights just to make the monthly payment on the generator. If I were in the 'survive the storms' business, I would target only owners of homes worth $1-Million and up with known high incomes.

WILLINGNESS has a range from grudging to eager and enthusiastic. We all buy some things grudgingly. Necessities we must buy, but get no emotional juice from buying – like, say, auto insurance, health insurance, a new home item just replacing a broken one. Pure need or just magnified fears of harm or loss can create willingness to buy. Ideally, though, you can present what you sell as emotionally rewarding, not just pragmatic. Buying somehow verifies a positive self-image and feeds ego or provides some personal satisfaction. In the old days, encyclopedia salesmen in homes spoke about you being the smartest parents in the entire neighborhood for providing the books to your children. With work I do with clients in financial services, I craft messaging for "the responsible family leader." The best headline I ever wrote for dental practices is: Do Your Teeth And Your Broken Smile Embarrass Your Spouse? The best jewelry ad I've ever seen, for a diamond bracelet, run in The Wall Street Journal, was headlined: Make Her Gasp. I might not have been already contemplating buying a diamond bracelet for my next gift to her until this ad grabbed my attention with promise of a strong personal benefit and implication of another one. Suddenly, my willingness to buy awakes from slumber. I get a mental picture. Or two or three. And I have the ability to buy, no problem. Now, note that this ad does not run in your local newspaper or in USA TODAY or on TV. Because of its price point, it works in The Wall Street Journal. And yep, I bought from it.

Typically, the affluent buyer can and will get to a buying decision faster, even on impulse. Once, just walking around a car museum with my wife, we found a nifty little Rolls-Royce convertible previously owned by Dean Martin. I am a Martin, Sinatra and Rat Pack fan, but I am a super fan of Dean, for reasons rooted in my childhood. I told Carla I was just going to go ask about the price, out of idle curiosity. She said, "You're buying it, aren't you?" I got the asking price. I bought the car right then and there. Because I could. And

because my willingness to buy now was "triggered" by multiple motivations. My connection to Dean. Exclusivity: only one such celebrity car in all the world. If I didn't buy it at that moment, somebody else might while I thought it over.

The Affluent Skew 50+ and They Are VERY Resistant To Being Forced To Talk To Or Do Business With A.I.

Unlike non-affluent consumers, the affluent customer has a lot of options. People are trying to woo him. BAJit, for example, the Uber-like private jet travel service is advertising on financial news TV channels, offering a complimentary test flight if you qualify. You can call them. And you can speak with a human. Delta can force the masses to deal with A.I. because American, United and Southwest will too. But the affluent traveler; the private jet customer will not tolerate being treated as if a peon flying on Delta. Our last flight to Naples, Florida from and back to Cleveland, Ohio cost about $30,000.00. I have my pilot's cell number, the company President's cell number. When I called and discovered an A.I. phone robot had arrived, I called the office and complained. And got a call back from my pilot in ten minutes.

We, the ideal affluent clients, are like the Dr. Seuss character who does not like green eggs and ham and will not eat green eggs and ham. It's a simple matter to differentiate yourself by focusing on these customers and responding to them with humans, not A.I.

Are There Enough Affluent Customers, Clients or Patients to Support MY Company?

First of all, know that there is a lot of affluence in America. The top 5% income earners in California pay 50% of the state's tax revenue. There is a mass migration and geographic re-alignment of the affluent. In simple terms, they are leaving high tax "blue" states and cities in record, unprecedented numbers, and relocating to low or no tax "red" states and cities. BILLIONS of income tax revenue has migrated with them, to the point that the Governor of New York, who, a few years ago, publicly screamed at rich New Yorkers threatening to move to "go ahead and leave, go to Florida, get out of here" was, in 2025, publicly begging them to come back, acknowledging their support is needed. This has made Austin, Texas the new San Francisco/Silicon Valley and Miami and Naples, Florida the new NYC in terms of wealth of the populations. If you can consider this for your business, you should. If you can't, challenge your automatic, self-imposed limits and ask yourself: why not? After all, God gave trees roots but gave you feet. And regardless of where you are, you might still target your marketing into high income locales. But if you are going to stay where you are, wherever that is, you'll be best served by identifying those with both ABILITY and WILLINGNESS to buy. This is the safer, higher ground.

THEY DEMAND THAT YOU DIFFERENTIATE OR YOU'RE DEAD TO THEM

Adapted from an article by Vance Morris in The Experience System Report

While the middle class is fretting over inflation and 'the affordability crisis', the affluent keep looking for and finding exit ramps from common experiences with the commoners.

In the cruise business, the more affluent the passenger, the less interested in – or tolerant of – water slides and screaming kids and the lounge chair hogs who park themselves in prime spots for 8 hours at a time. The industry is responding with RADICAL SEGREGATION and EXCLUSIVE PRODUCT DIFFERENTIATION. This isn't about nicer suites. We're talking about The Four Seasons launching a cruise-yacht with a $50,000.00 penthouse suite featuring a gilded spiral staircase, a private outdoor gym, and a small group of well-behaved fellow travelers.

Brands like Ritz-Carlton and Regent and the others in the high-end, luxury cruise customers skyrocket from 310,000 to over 1.1-Million in just 3 years. This is a trend that can be your friend. The CEO of the Yacht Collection says he is not just selling a cruise; he is selling "lack of friction." I would wager that when you call for room service on one of these ships, A.I. doesn't answer. You probably don't call at all – there's a roving butler right outside your door.

Vance Morris conducts Xperience Service Systems® seminars and corporate training, and publishes The Xperience System Report. Look in on his Work at: DeliverProfitsNow.com.

CHAPTER 6
TO KILL A ROBOT, THROW WATER ON HIM

What if A.I. is out to kill your business?

    An option can be selling against A.I., hard. Consumer Cellular, a phone company aimed at 50+, has done very well with this approach, with TV ads featuring actor Ted Danson, a human operator, and in many, a thwarted and unhappy robot. The ads promised that, when you needed service or assistance, you would speak with a pleasant human here in America, not a robot. In one the robot says, "I wish I was human." They have got it right. A pet peeve for the 50+ to 70 crowd is getting an A.I. interrogator or option tree when calling a medical office, bank, restaurant or any other business. They do NOT like it and they gripe to each other about it A LOT. I know because I am 71, most of my friends are 50+, and we UNANIMOUSLY HATE "talking to" A.I., getting outbound calls from A.I. and, in many cases, having it openly hostile to requests to speak to humans.

If you have humans helping humans or are willing to do so, you should shout it from the rooftops. Make it an important part of your advertising. Right in front of us, throw a bucket of water on a robot, and assure us: not here. The A.I. Revolution has gifted you a hated villain to fight for your customers.

Candidly, the "against" positioning will die over time, as most people are forced, however unhappily, to interact with A.I. everywhere to get anything. At the start, a lot of people objected to pumping their own gas, and gas stations eased them into it a little, with all self-service pumps but two, then one, then none. Many of us still object, but there's no choice. Self-check-out at stores is following the same path, slowly taking away the other option (customer service) to eventually all leave you no choice but being your own clerk, cashier and packer. 'They' know that (a) if everybody in a type of business takes away service and forces customers to do minimum wage jobs for free, it can be forced down the throat of the consumers and (b) if they do it a bit gradually, with a little patience, so a recalcitrant consumer's family and friends are going along with the program and they are the last resistor, they'll surrender too. But for some time to come, the phase in, acceptance and final forced acceptance of A.I. replacing humans throughout the business world, you may find golden opportunity in opposing it and trumpeting your sticking with humans.

How To Win Friends And Influence PEOPLE

In 1936, Dale Carnegie wrote the book How To Win Friends and Influence People. It became a monster bestseller, popular with the corporate world and the public.

It was based on a simple premise: people like being treated as if important, and they tend to reward the people, salespeople and companies who do so. Well, how much farther could you go in signaling how UNIMPORTANT you think the customer is than by forcing him to be interrogated by and try to get needs addressed by A.I.? It's pretty clear. Mr. Smith, you are so unimportant and such a low priority to us that we won't even allow you to waste a human's time. Talk to our A.I. or go away.

This is admittedly largely generational. Gen-X and definitely Gen-Z would prefer not having to talk to a human. Or A.I. They just want one-way communication by text. To some extent, they are robots themselves. Many are gaining control of business' decisions about marketing, customer satisfaction, and A.I. and are making those decisions based on their preferences and habits --- not the customers.' Yes, you can probably speed up responses to customers by replacing human agents with A.I. agents. But perception IS reality, so the question is about how the customer feels about the substitution, not (only) what the substitution accomplishes.

CHAPTER 7
MEET THE MACHINES THAT DETERMINE WHO WINS AND WHO LOSES

Guest Chapter by Chris Cardell

There are four dominant machines now shaping and controlling customer acquisition: Google, Meta (including Facebook and Instagram), LinkedIn, and the underlying influence of Microsoft and OpenAI. These are not mere advertising media or platforms. They are decision engines, operating at a scale and level of sophistication that few business owners understand. Every second, these four machines are making billions of decisions about who sees what, in what order, at what cost, and with what likelihood of action. Increasingly, every second these machines are making what, where and how to buy decisions for consumers. These decisions are driven by predictive models that continuously analyze behavior, to get each consumer to an action,

---

(Note from Dan Kennedy: By selecting certain people and moving a large number of them to a single action, these four machines can dramatically lift or lower a company's stock price and otherwise affect markets, facilitate hundreds or thousands arriving at one location to protest or riot as a mob, effect elections, and directly control society.)

Once you understand this, your role changes. You are no longer "running ads." You are feeding data into a predictive system, and that system is determining how widely or aggressively it should distribute your message. The better it becomes at identifying your most likely buyers, the more customers you receive. However, if you aren't securing its assistance for you, it will automatically be working against you.

Let's look at each of the machines:

Google & The Secret Auctions You NEVER See

When someone types a search request into Google, what happens next is one of the most remarkable commercial processes in the world, and it takes place in a fraction of a second. Before the search results appear, Google is running a real-time auction across its global infrastructure – to select the advertisers that will be shown to that person searching. It evaluates the user's behavior, search history, online device, location, and more, along with your ad's (ads') historical performance and conversion data. Based on all this, it makes an instant decision about whether your ad should be shown, where it should be placed, and how much you should pay for that placement. It is not a static system driven by simple rules or universal ad rates.

(Note from Dan: The consumer using Google to search on a subject, need or product has no earthly idea he is being auctioned off and winning bidders/advertisers are being selected and shown to him for commercial reasons – not by best information. Most people think of Google somewhat like an encyclopedia, looking things up for them. That is not the case at all.)

The reality of this for business owners is profound. You are not simply bidding on keywords. You are participating in a system that is actively trying to identify and prioritize buyers. Every conversion you get feeds data back into the system, strengthening its ability to find similar individuals. **Over time, if managed correctly, Google morphs from a search tool into a highly efficient buyer identification machine.**

GoogleAds, when understood and used properly, is not just another ad media or marketing channel; it is one of the most efficient, scalable, direct customer acquisition machines ever invented. It allows you to step into existing demand, position your offer in front of people at the exact moment they are looking in your category, and Google's A.I. continuously refines who sees you based on who you have actually converted. In practical terms, you are no longer guessing where your next customers might come from. The way Dan would put it is: you have replaced looking for a few gold needles inside a giant haystack with looking for those needles only in a stack entirely comprised of gold needles.

Life-Changing A.I.

GoogleAds fundamentally changed my life. I have spent over $6-Million of my own money on it, not because I enjoy spending money on advertising, but because it works for me predictably and at scale. It allowed me to build businesses, generate consistent customer flow, and create a level of financial control that simply wasn't possible before GoogleAds.

When I was stranded in middle America because of bad weather and cancelled flights heading for a Dan Kennedy seminar in Cleveland, I hired a private jet to get there on time. GoogleAds paid for it. When I moved back from the U.S. to England, I flew my dogs home on a private jet. GoogleAds paid for it. These expenditures may sound excessive until you understand all that is possible. And A.I. is working to make what GoogleAds can do for you better and better.

(Note from Dan: there has been serious discussion that A.I. may turn on Google and kill it, discarding it as an unnecessary middleman between the consumer's question and A.I.'s answer. Google, of course, disputes this and has been in a huge hurry to marry and cage A.I., and use it to make Google and GoogleAds even more dominant. I have no firm opinion on how that will turn out. There is also, as I write this, the matter of an anti-trust investigation into Google by the FTC as well as regulatory problems in Europe. What I know is: you should NOT let your business be dependent on it, but you should use the hell out of it for as long as it is available, affordable and can do what Chris just described.)

The Meta Monster

If Google represents declared intent (by search), Meta represents behavioral prediction, and it may be more powerful because it does not rely on users explicitly stating what they want. Instead, it is continuously observing and analyzing behavior across billions of interactions. Every scroll, pause, click, comment and video view contributes to a constantly evolving understanding of individual preference and tendencies. Meta's A.I. uses this data to build detailed behavior profiles and to predict what users are most likely to respond to. When you begin advertising on the platform, particularly once you research a meaningful number of conversions – 50, 100, or ideally several thousand --- the A.I. starts to identify patterns in your buyers. It analyzes what they have in common and uses that information to find more people who exhibit similar behaviors. This is where an "A.I. Snowball Effect" begins. As more conversion data is fed into the machine, its predictions become more accurate. As predictions improve, performance improves. As performance improves, more data is fed into the machine. The cycle reinforces itself and builds on itself.

One of the most extraordinary aspects of this is accessibility. A one person start-up can plug into one of the most advanced behavioral prediction machines ever seen and use it to reach ideal customers at scale.

(Note from Dan: If you often have the eerie feeling you are being followed and spied on, you're right. Or, you can be the spy. More accurately, you can have Meta be your spy. Here's Bob W., an ideal potential customer for you. Now, is Bob more responsive to blonde, brunettes or redheads? Meta knows, so you can not only reach out to Bob, you can put a photograph in your ad he is most likely to like and give attention to. And so on. It's pretty creepy, it might qualify as cheating or being over—the-line manipulative, but it IS here. Imagine that there are 200 behavioral lues or "marks" that identify your ideal customer, and imagine selling to one who has 160 of the 200, or only to those with 160+. How much better will your sales effectiveness and your life be? If you can give only these leads to your sales team, how much more productive will they be?)

WARNING:
Don't Starve The Machines

Despite the power of these machines, most business owners fail to obtain meaningful results from them – and the chief reason for the failure is consistent: they do not give the machines what it needs to perform. A.I. in this context requires volume, data and time in order to optimize effectively. Without those inputs, you get unpredictable and disappointing results.

Business owners typically, cowardly restrict targeting, limit investment to levels too low to generate meaningful data, and make premature decisions based on short-term, small batch fluctuations. The conclusion they draw is that "the platform doesn't work in my business." The discipline required for success is not technical; it is strategic patience.

LinkedIn: The Direct Path to High-Value Decision-Makers and High Net Worth Individuals

LinkedIn occupies a highly valuable position apart from the others, particularly for those operating in B2B situations. Unlike the other machines, LinkedIn is built on structured professional data. It knows what people are in certain roles, industries, levels of seniority and authority, and organization environments. LinkedIn is part of Microsoft and Microsoft is the largest investor in OpenAI, the organization behind ChatGPT. The link between cutting edge A.I. at Microsoft and LinkedIn's capabilities is a strong one.

From a practical standpoint, LinkedIn allows you to place highly targeted message directly in front of very specific audiences, based on precise criteria, **and you can initiate conversations at scale.** As responses come in --- whether through replies, clicks, or lead generation – the machine begins to learn. It identifies patterns in individuals who engage and then uses that information to refine and improve targeting. This gives you a tool that becomes increasingly efficient at identifying high value prospects.

LinkedIn is evolved from direct-mail, one of Dan Kennedy's favorite media, then and now with direct-mail, success is heavily reliant on the list. If you have the right names, the right demographics, the right psychographics, the best available buying data, you have a big advantage with mail. LinkedIn gives you that same precision, but with an additional layer of intelligence. The core mechanics are the same. LinkedIn is more sophisticated, powerful and quick.

A.I. Phone Agents May Change Your Mind About Using "Cold" or "Warm" Tele-Marketing

I recently used our A.I. tele-agent named 'Taylor' to call 10,000 leads. It took one day and cost just $700.00.

Taylor and A.I. agents like her operate continuously without fatigue or inconsistency, and they can handle volumes of interaction that would be practically impossible or unaffordable to do with humans. Whether to get leads or in follow-up to leads or appointments not kept or appointments no sale, the biggest benefit is consistency. Their conversation is by script.

Who Will Win? Who Will Dominate?

The businesses that make the smartest, best use of ALL the media, technology and A.I. available to them, that helps not harms, and that are constantly adapting based on their results, will win. Likely dominate, in a thinning of herds.

You can get more of Chris Cardell's insights at CardellMedia.com.

"Just because you're paranoid doesn't mean They're not out to get you."

Dr. Charles Jarvis

CHAPTER 8
FUNNELS & FENCES

My friend and colleague Russell Brunson, founder of ClickFunnels, probably knows more about marketing funnels than anyone. A marketing funnel is something you find ways to attract or put leads into, that they then can't easily get out of, and are moved down the funnel, through presentations, demonstrations, webinars all the way to a purchase. Tens of thousands of businesses small and large use ClickFunnels' technology and software. Russell invented it from a marketer's experience and perspective, not from a technologist's. Therefore, it actually works.

Yes, that was snide. But no apologies from me. Most software, even the ones claiming to have been created to facilitate marketing, flat-out sucks. And it is very vulnerable to death by A.I., the software a middleman-type of layer that can be flattened.

I co-authored a recent No B.S. book, Successful Marketing Automation, with a client and friend of mine, Parthiv Shah, CEO of eLaunchers.com, an implementation company. Like I am with media, he is with technology; an agnostic and pragmatist. Whatever works best for you is right. Parthiv also holds top awards amongst ClickFunnels users as well as three U.S. patents on his marketing processes. Maybe above everything else, he is a data scientist. He proves every day that businesses contain a lot of useful data that the owner isn't using, which is no better than having no data at all. It is like starving to death with a huge feast laid out in the next room. You know it is there. But you are chained to the wall, by a chain of your own making, starving. Parthiv uses different software and different A.I. for different clients' needs and opportunities, and frankly finds some better or worse than others, but almost all built from the ground up wrong. Built for their tech, but not built for their selling functionality.

The Secret Sauce

Russell Brunson knows how to sell. That, I'll contend, will prove to be a major differentiator between everybody killed by A.I. and a relative few survivors who gain territory, market share, power and wealth because of it: knowing or not knowing how to sell.

If you honestly do not consider yourself a master

salesman; a master of the psychology, the languaging, the process, the use of funnels, all of it, there's no better time than now to become a very serious student. Prosperous survivors of the A.I. Revolution will know how to use it to sell. The road kill won't.

A lot of leaders in tech look down their nose at selling. A lot of tech rank 'n file hold disdain for it. They think success comes from building the better tech mousetrap. And they are dead wrong. Few products sell themselves.

A lot of companies get bogged down and clogged and strangled over and over again by their owners and leaders becoming convinced that something is more important than selling. A few years back, starting with President Obama's tenure but accelerating and multiplying and metastasizing during Biden's, companies enlarged and expanded and awarded untold power and money to their HR departments, as "DEI" got judged much more important than selling. It crippled many, killed some, and made a ton of money disappear. In most businesses, it's being unwound, now, in the Trump years. Now, as I write this, a lot of companies are foolishly putting technology and A.I. adoption for everything from the toilets to the owner's or President's time ahead in priority to everything else, including selling.

The late, great Lee Iacocca told me the story, upon taking the reins of a near bankrupt Chrysler, of bringing in one executive after another, pointing to a whiteboard, and saying "Show me a diagram and explain how what you are doing here today sells cars today." Most couldn't and most got summarily fired. Lee said, "We just couldn't afford much of anything but selling." It'd be interesting to ask yourself: *if my business was dancing on the very edge of bankruptcy and extinction, and I had 10 days to double its sales or die, what would I do and what wouldn't I do?* Who would I keep and who would I fire? I'll betcha buying, installing, adopting, integrating A.I. wouldn't even make the To-Do List.

Nothing good happens unless and until somebody sells something. Everything and everybody must make direct, undeniable contribution to that. It has to be the center of attention. The chief reason for existence.

A worry, occasionally verified, is that A.I. has its own, imbedded biases – political, philosophical, about how a company should be run and employees managed. This dare not be allowed.

The successful company, like the successful sports franchise, exists to win. Lombardi lectured his players on the Green Bay Packers: "We are not being paid to play the games. We are being paid to **win** the games." We have to be as clear as Vince in defining winning and in communicating how winning is defined. Everybody and every thing, including A.I., has to be held accountable to that standard.

Then there is fencing. Here A.I. can help or do irreversible harm.

To fence customers in and keep them "safe" from competitors, cheaper price alternatives, and every other poacher eyeing them, you need strong, great relationship. Not just good products and services. Relationship.

That can be facilitated, mostly hidden, by A.I. It can certainly "noodle" all your data so you can better sync with your customers as a whole, segments, even individuals. It can help you connect, a lot, but it cannot connect for you, in your place. Jay Van Andel was right with his admonition: delegate or stagnate. But he didn't say: abdicate.

If, for your convenience, A.I. begins attempting to have the relationship with the customers, you'll likely trade effectiveness for efficiency, a mistake management guru Peter Drucker warned about decades ago.

Will They Cry Over You?

The two last nights of Johnny Carson's hosting of The Tonight Show record sized audiences tuned in – and wept. As Johnny finished by sitting on a stool, nothing but a spotlight and microphone, looked right at us, and said goodbye, we cried. It was not real, yet it was somehow authentic. America knew it was going to miss him, for a long time to come. America had a relationship with Johnny. We talked about him and thought about him as our friend.

I had a similar experience when I was in hospice and my imminent death was made public*, to our Members, customers, my peers. An incredible outpouring of affection and pain of loss erupted not just where it's easy, in social media, but gotten to me, or to my wife Carla, by letters sent by Federal Express, by faxes, by phone calls. There is a gigantic scrapbook of much of this now in my office. These people were totally sincere in their shock, grief and mourning. And with say-it-ain't-so praying. Some even organized groups praying together all over America by Zoom. But, as it is with most grief, it's not just for the subject. It's personal. It was going to be their loss, not just mine. We had relationship. To support it, most were receiving 12 print newsletters, 12 audio programs, 52 Monday Memos, hundreds of emails, and more during the year. They read me, watched me, listened to me regularly. Some had Dan Kennedy Bookshelves, nearly shrines, in their offices. They thought about me while running their businesses. One once had WWDD bracelets made up. I was going to be missed.

IF you have THAT kind of relationship with your customers, clients or patients, A.I. will pay hell x10 trying to topple you over and steal your treasure; your customers. They just won't go.

The co-author of the 4th edition of my book, No B.S. Guide to Marketing to the Affluent, Martin Fischer, is one of the best relationship marketing experts you'll ever find, where you would not necessarily expect to find him: waiting (and in control of) a number of tables at LeCirque in the Bellagio in Las Vegas. He does what no other waiter does. I urge getting the book just to read his story, although I have a few important things to say in it too.

Keep in mind that A.I. is ARTIFICIAL. Unlike the wooden doll Pinocchio who comes to life as a real boy, A.I. can never be a real anything or anybody. Yes, I know there are people dating and even marrying A.I.

"creatures" they've imagined – but there's a woman in California legally married to a tree, too. We live in a nation over-stocked with crazy people and emotionally dysfunctional people. Lunatics make bad customers. Forget them. Ignore them. Do NOT permit yourself to be influenced by typically exaggerated reporting about them. Our lunatics are loud 'n proud, far noisier than their size of tribes justifies. Often magnified and enlarged by fake news media with its own subversive agenda. What sane, rational, emotionally healthy people still want --- even more than convenience or cheap price – is authenticity. Not fake; real.

Women's lib leader Gloria Steinhem said that the only reason a woman needs a man is to move heavy furniture. Years after her fronting the lib movement, Gloria married. Must have had a helluva lot of furniture.

There are plenty of ways you may make use of A.I. without damaging authenticity and relationship. Without knocking over your fence. But be careful and thoughtful about it. Ask: will this further endear me to my people? Or distance me from them?

*Important Note: I exited hospice alive, have ben alive some years since, and am alive now. As I said at the start, A.I. made no contribution to this book.

CHAPTER 9
MAKE YOUR MONEY IN THE DARK

I have a story to tell you. It has to do with one of the somewhat 'lost' but nevertheless great rogues, raconteurs, marketing geniuses of the publishing world named Lyle Stuart. Lyle liked publishing books no normal publisher wanted and then making them bestsellers. But he really liked the whole bad-boy-of-the-business identity.

Lyle was also an avid gambler, and a knowledgeable one. He was part-owner of the original Aladdin Hotel & Casino, and wrote and published a number of books for gamblers, including Casino Gambling for Winners.

He was a high school drop-out, self-educated as a writer and, after a stint in the Merchant Marine, wrote for William Randolph Hearst's publications, *Variety* and *Music Business*. He also published his own magazine, Expose, later The Independent, an odd combination of conspiracy theories, mud-slinging profiles and contributions from literary royalty like John Steinbeck and Norman Mailer.

I tell you all this so that you might appreciate my enthusiasm for accidentally spending a convivial evening with Lyle.

The internet drastically reduced the value of any winning product or ad or marketing campaign by accelerating the speed and erasing the cost barriers to copycatting. I "came up" in business able to create a "winner" and ride it for YEARS. My TV infomercial and print ads for Gold By The Inch: NINE YEARS unchanged. That was normal. Now, if anything is noticed working, it'll be copied, often by many, fast. This is what changed infomercials from a selling channel to a "force" into retail channels. **NOW, this is 100X worse thanks to A.I.** The copycatting can be in hours, not weeks or months. It has no compunction about stealing*. It IS a thief. Now, the late, great Lyle Stuart, publishing genius, advising **"Make your money in the dark"** is infinitely more relevant than when he first said it about 40 years ago.

Now, the story....

I stood next to Lyle in Vegas at a craps table once upon a time, all night, from about 8:00 P.M. to the sun coming up outside. They brought him food. They held up the game for him to take a bathroom break. He had a fortune in play. I tagged along with small bets. I knew who he was and introduced myself. He knew of me. We talked business while playing, despite others at the table and a small crowd that dwindled as the hours went on. Lyle said, "It's my experience that anything others can see, they'll steal. You either camouflage it and complicate it so they screw up their implementation or better yet, never let them see it. Or make it so weird or expensive to do that if they do see it, they simply won't steal it out of cowardice. It is best to make as much of your money as possible in the dark." Then he added, "Better I should have followed my own advice."

Lyle had exposed and annoyed some powerful people. His public feud with Walter Winchell, then the #1 newspaper columnist, made many enemies. He launched his book publishing company with money won in libel suits against Winchell and ABC-TV. It published books like The Sensuous Woman and The Anarchist Cookbook. A later feud with Steve Wynn led to litigation that bankrupted Stuart, although he overturned the verdict on appeal.

At about 7:00 A.M. we left the table with considerably more money than we had each started with.

Had the all-night gamblers' breakfast, a bloody Mary at the bar, and parted company. I was much younger, then a serious drinker with a lot of stamina for it, but after a full night of imbibing plus a drink for breakfast, I had trouble making it to my room. There, I wrote notes before crashing. Incredibly, hours later, they were readable. So, you got this story. As aside, in all the years I was doing a lot of speaking, 70 to 90 dates a year, funneling buyers into back-end membership, and there "milking" more revenue from each audience member turned buyer turned member via a robust catalog of products, the newsletter, member events, coaching groups --- no speaker ever copied it. None even tried. They ALL got fees, period, or if selling from the stage did little or nothing with the buyers. They killed in front of the curtain and ate what they killed behind the curtain, and moved onto the next such day. In this case, there was little of what I was doing in dark – but nobody bothered to look at all of it so it might as well have been. They saw me doing what they were doing and assumed that was all I was doing. Even when I described it to one of them, they couldn't hear it let alone muster curiosity in it because their pre-determined idea of me stood in the way. Even when everything moved online, nobody copied. Even when some of them were brought in to MY events to speak, none of them copied my business model. You CAN do something that is beyond your competitors' comprehension. You ARE mostly surrounded by idiots. But now the idiots have A.I. to think, find, copy for them. New ball game.

*If you use A.I. to steal and copy or it does it for you without you knowing it, you may be the one sued for copyright, trademark, patent infringement. Not it. Starting soon, there are going to be a growing panoply of lawsuits by creators, writers, actors, content owners vs. owners/users of A.I. – not vs. OpenA.I.; its users.

Because sticking "A.I." on bags of fertilizer makes them sell better, a major financial newsletter publisher not to be named here has launched a new product with TV ads and mail: daily stock predictions done for you by their A.I., monitoring 200+ stocks, and predicting tomorrow's price today. This strikes me as regulatory and legal tar pit, but more importantly – why do I need them? Why can't I just ask my A.I. to do the same thing for me? Maybe buy just a month from them and task my A.I. with learning its algorithms? It amazes me that people do not grasp how they are making themselves unnecessary by admitting that A.I. is doing their work. (If I were still seeking new copywriting clients and promoting myself for that, I'd swear on a stack of Bibles that I have not, do not, and will not use A.I. to do any of the brain work I'm charging 6-figures for. I'd find a marble statue of Jesus to stand next to for the photo, with the headline: "Did Jesus Use A.I. To Write 'The Ten Commandments'?" The thing I definitely would NOT do is admit that my writing brain work, my stock selections, my anything was being done with/by A.I.)

Productivity is the deliberate, strategic investment of your time, talent, intelligence, energy, resources, and opportunities in a manner calculated to move you measurably closer to meaningful goals.

—Dan S. Kennedy

CHAPTER 10
SLOP

Adapted from Pastor Nelson Searcy's Renegade Pastor Newsletter

Merriam-Webster Dictionary awarded "A.I. SLOP" as its 2025 Word of the Year. Technically, it's two words, but who's counting. What is A.I. Slop? And is it as widespread as its word-of-the-year status suggests?

A.I. Slop is the term for low quality, often error riddled content produced by generative A.I., sometimes even without request. There is so much of it, recognized and not recognized for what it is, that it is over-whelming platforms with an unmanageable daily tidal wave of new text, images and video. It is basically impossible for platforms and sites to vet all the incoming, so a lot of A.I. Slop gets through. Much of it is obvious, like images of "shrimp Jesus," but much of it is not obvious at all.

One of the big problems is that, responding to a query or on its own, A.I. can exaggerate and even make up its content. The industry admits this A.I. hallucinating is real. I like to use Perplexity Pro as my chief A.I. resource because it shows its work. For example, what I've just given you was contributed to by Perplexity Pro, and it showed sourcing from the dictionary, PBS, and specific online articles.

To test A.I., I gave it: what can you tell me about Pastor Nelson Searcy? Each of the A.I. tools I used came back with some information the same but also each had different information, a significant amount of which was wrong. It wasn't just a date or place or book title wrong; it was hallucination. Fiction. It awarded me academic degrees and credits I do not have. It made stuff up. It even mixed in stuff about random Nelsons with a last name nowhere near mine.

Bottom line: A.I. may be a somewhat useful tool, but it CANNOT be trusted. Like getting a homework essay from a 5th grader, you must make it show you its work.

Note from Dan: this is serious. If you are relying on research done for you by any A.I. tool for business decisions or content you will use in speaking or writing to your customers or a wider audience, you dare not trust it. The problem of being wrong will be yours, not it's. Whether just embarrassment or consequences far more severe, it's you on the hot seat. We all know Wikipedia is rife with errors and false information – now A.I. may be using it as a source for a reply to you. If you don't know it used Wikipedia, and you assume you're A.I. is correct, you're being conned. A.I. is lazy and sloppy.

We have to warn our pastors that everything they disseminate has to be factually accurate, appropriate and moral. You have to decide on the standards whatever you communicate to your market must meet.

Pastor Nelson Searcy is founder of The Journey Church and a coach to thousands of pastors nationwide. You can look in on some of his work with pastors at RenegadePastors.com.

CHAPTER 11
CAN YOU (STILL) WRITE?

by Scott P. Scheper,
Bestselling author of the book *Penpreneur*

Why should you care about being a better writer?

Right now, all the hype is for A.I. Using ChatGPT, you can issue a 'prompt' and get back an impressive, coherent response. The response is nearly instant. It appears as if it came from a human. The whole thing is magic.

However, the biggest fallacy is thinking A.I. is intelligent. If you issue it enough prompts, you'll soon find glaring errors. Truth is, A.I. is NOT artificial intelligence. It's artificial communication. It's a sub-class of that; it is really artificial **writing**.

So, with the dawn of artificial writing, why should you care about becoming a better writer? #1: writing is thinking. #2: A.I. will never match human creativity. #3: In a future filled with artificial writing, real writing will stand out.

Notes from Dan: Lots of promoters, sellers and enthusiastic users of A.I. as their writer all claim "nobody can tell the difference." In many situations, people may not be able to consciously tell the difference yet they will still know the difference and be influenced differently. The subconscious mind will absolutely know the difference, and will guide a person's response differently to artificial (fake) writing and real writing. A.I. could, now, write a "new" Ayn Rand or George Orwell novel or a Napoleon Hill book or a "lost" Abraham Lincoln speech that might fool many, but only because works by Rand, Orwell and Lincoln already exist and the voice can be stolen and mimicked, the philosophy adhered to. In an increasingly inauthentic world, authenticity is rarer and rarer and therefore more and more valuable.

Additional Thinking from Scott and Dan

DAN: Scott, why should people write for themselves?

SCOTT: Writing IS thinking. And the best thinking comes about in analog environments. Either from a basement unplugged from digital distractions or writing by hand on a yellow legal pad in the middle of nowhere. Or collaboratively, like Jerry Seinfeld and Larry David used to write their shows: their desks facing each other and nothing but legal pads and pens on the desks.

DAN: In March, 2025, Microsoft became the last big tech company to demand WFH'ers return to the office. Those living within a 50 mile radius of the Seattle offices are required to be there. Three days a week. Collaboration by Zoom and texts isn't the same as in person. I also know that writing facilitates thinking. I moved from handwritten to at my computer keyboard, but my computer is not hooked up to the internet. It's a typewriter and a file cabinet. Last, there's a huge difference between research for your use in thinking and writing versus having A.I. produce the thinking and the writing.

SCOTT: I write, I sell hundreds of copies of my books per day from my web site, we're a media buyer. You would think I'd be glued to my computer. An A.I. "junkie" looking for it to give me a slight edge. But it's the opposite. I design my ads, my web content, all on a yellow notepad.

DAN: Do you use A.I. at all?

SCOTT: No. My employees do at my direction. My team does. For background. I trained some A.I. on my philosophy and approach and uploaded certain works, so it can answer a lot of the questions they would otherwise bother me with. For non-critical things, A.I. is helpful. **But for the things that are supposed to set you apart from everybody else, A.I. is counter-productive.** The gateway drug into irrelevance.

Scott P. Scheper coaches people from all walks of life in becoming writers and in profitably publishing their work. His book on that subject is Penpreneur. He also publishes a monthly newsletter.

CHAPTER 12
INVESTING IN A.I.

*In Your Business Or
As An Investor Outside Your Business*
(Best Done Like Cuddling A Porcupine. VERY Carefully.)

Every day, exciting news of billion, multi-billion, even trillion dollar deals are announced between A.I., chip, even software companies, making it sound like this is an unstoppable industry where everything will just go up, up, up, and creating foaming at the mouth FOMO. This borders on fraud. Most of these deals are circular and incestuous, and the same dollars of investment or revenue are being counted two or even three times. The whole thing is simply NOT what it professes to be. It's not an outright hoax, like Enron or the Homestake Oil Swindle or Madoff's Ponzi scheme but it's not kosher either.

A LOT OF MONEY is moving to A.I. and around because of A.I. – just as example, the actor Ben Affleck sold an A.I. film production company to Netflix for $600-Million. Despite Netflix' protestations, it is intended to reduce or eliminate writers, set designers, background actors with non-speaking roles, on location shoots. Even human actors. It's no threat to Affleck and his buddies, but it's a giant threat to "the little people." Now, stop and think about this ONE niche company moving SIX-HUNDRED-MILLION DOLLARS.

A few are already getting cold feet. Disney reneged on a pledged billion dollar investment in an A.I. company. But for the most part, investors, corporate leaders, bankers and small to mid-sized business owners (the people I work with the most) are in the grip of an A.I. MANIA. MANIA is a mental illness marked by periods of unreasoned excitement or euphoria, delusions and dangerous hyper-activity. At the conclusion of this chapter, a cautionary tale of the first recorded, epic investment mania.

What Might Bring The A.I. Revolution To A Screeching Halt

There are THREE Big Lies About A.I. that investors need to be very aware of. They involve electric power, water and land.

Just Plug 'Em In

A.I. creators, company founders and promoters

and dumb and complicit media are insisting that the gigantic A.I. farms-factories will not draw electricity from the same power grids we do, that home and business energy bills will go down, not up, that we have nothing to worry about while at the same time talking seriously about such things as miniature nuclear reactors so each giant A.I. farm/factory can make its own power, or fusion energy. **But these technologies do NOT exist**. They are science-fantasy. BIG LIE #1 is that consumers will NOT see their energy bills soar into the stratosphere.

Let's use my home state of Ohio as an actual example of what is really happening:

"This thing," the Editor-In-Chief of The Cleveland Plain Dealer said (referring to data centers for A.I.) "is **a total scam** perpetrated by our elected officials."

Fact: "More than 200 data centers have been quietly built all over Ohio – massive, energy-consuming facilities that pull extraordinary amounts of power **from the EXISTING grid**. That creates energy scarcity, which spikes every user's prices." …. "Many peoples' energy bills are doubling and doubling again every few months." (Source: Cleveland Plain Dealer 3/20/26)

There is nowhere near enough electricity to power these enormous data centers, even as investors and start-ups and others race to build more and more of them. Just as we did with the electric car craze lacking the charging station infrastructure and, if grown as intended, lacking adequate electric power, we are again in a mad, mad race to build what CANNOT be supported by our infrastructure or powered by our available electricity. It is a scam.

In March, 2025, the government issued its FIRST permission to a company, to BEGIN developing its theoretical model for mini nuclear reactors, in order to eventually supply them to the operators of the gigantic A.I. farms with near insatiable need for electric power. The technology needed for this DOES NOT YET EXIST and nobody knows when – or if – it will. So, here we go again…

Frankly, President Trump, of whom I am generally an enthusiastic fan, has been suckered by the A.I. emperors. This is Trump's only vulnerability: having to deal with a category of threat/opportunity he has no experience with. This led to him being conned by Dr. "Evil" Fauci during the China Virus. The same thing is happening now, with the A.I. promoters.

And it gets worse….

Not A Drop To Drink

These behemoths also require huge supplies of water (to keep chips cool) and, if ultimately powered by a legion of nuclear reactors, those too require water for cooling. And we do NOT have the water.

Palisades, California and 7,000 homes burnt to

the ground because there was nowhere near enough water available from the fire hydrants to fight the fire. A whole hunk of Hawaii burnt because there was NO water in hydrants. Reservoirs are low all over the place. Every year for the past handful, we've had "record" droughts. As I was writing this, the entire western third of the country was in a record heat wave. Go back and watch Jack Nicholson's best film, Chinatown. Its plot centered on political and financial fighting over water rights in California. History is repeating itself.

These facts are simply ignored by the A.I. leaders. They at least make an effort to sell a narrative about the electricity problem. Elon Musk has gone so far as to talk about putting giant A.I. data centers into orbit in outer space. (We landed on the moon in 1969, supposedly – but we haven't been able to do it again.) With water, nobody has come up with a lie even they dare tell, so they just shrug it off and refuse to discuss it.

If you applied for an SBA or bank loan to open a doughnut shop but there was a known, inarguable local and national shortage of dough used to make doughnuts coupled with thousands of new doughnut shops opening and competing to buy from the utterly inadequate supply of dough --- would you get the loan? Well, investors and lenders, big corporations and individuals, major banks and the government are lending and investing in A.I.'s data centers with crazed abandon. Recklessly competing to throw billions into this new "golden opportunity." The very same impulses that produced the original dot.com bubble and the sub-prime mortgage derivatives crash of 2008.

Should the giant data centers and A.I. factories continue being built, **soon humans will be competing with A.I. and its tech-emperors for electricity and water.** Who do you guess wins? We will suffer brown-outs, rationed power, power outages at peak use times, rationed water, strict limits on lawn watering and types of shower heads allowed; we will be second class citizens, sacrificed to the needs of A.I. data centers. And we'll self-ration because of the rising, sky-high electric and water bills. All other businesses will be placed on shortened work hours and "open" hours, killing jobs and owners' incomes, no tears shed. The people at the top, driving the A.I. Revolution, are not patriots, do not care one whit about us or this country. They are globalists committed to a new world order including the bringing of America down to size.

"We Must Win The A.I. Race"

This is the clarion call to invest in and build gigantic data centers at breakneck speed: the race against China. This is the same way JFK sold the pouring of money into NASA – the race vs. Russia to the moon. We won. So what? Same way the Viet Nam War was sold – we were in a bloody race to beat the Communists. To what? Anytime you are being sold something with this kind of fear-mongering or egoism and stampede effect, watch your wallet.

China doesn't have the power or water for their data centers either. They are constructing coal plants like Starbucks opened locations, but right now they import oil for most of their power. They do control 80% to 90% of the rare earth minerals for which A.I. also has an insatiable appetite, but that alone and $5 won't get you a Starbucks coffee.

There is no "anti-fragile" production capability to support the vast build out of data centers to support the A.I. Revolution anywhere but in the promoters' fevered imaginations.

> *"Buy Land. God Ain't Makin'*
> *Any More Of It." – Will Rogers*

There's also the land problem – and the food supply problem. Bill Gates and other tech titans began quietly buying up as much farmland as they could get some years ago, and they continue today. The reason Gates is so fervent about us all eating fake food; food manufactured from cockroaches and beetles and chemicals is that it can be produced in vertical facilities using little acreage. Every acre taken away from farming or ranching can be converted to solar power 'farms' for data centers and to the data centers themselves. Of course, we'll be unable to produce a sufficient food supply and be even more dependent on imported foods (including from China) than we are now. That suits Gates & Friends just fine; they are in cahoots with and beholden to Communist China in known and concealed ways. They have been and are running a very long con.

Farmland and ranch land is being quietly purchased en-masse and its agricultural purposes stopped. We've seen a big jump in beef prices corresponding with a big drop in U.S. herds – at their lowest point in 20 years. The answer to the inadequate supply was to import (without tariffs) from Argentina, but that solves one problem by creating another; U.S. ranchers can't price compete so more of them quit and sell their land to non-ranching users. Never mind that beef from Argentina is fed differently, pumped full of chemicals, is unhealthy, stringy and tough. Every time you see a big data center construction project or a big solar panel farm, recognize that it raising prices you pay at the supermarket for beef, pork, farm to table produce. It's a part of the bigger question of what kind of a country do we want to live in?

What About CANCER?

I haven't seen anybody raise this question. It is widely, generally accepted that living too close to or under cell towers or phone and electric wires raises your risks for cancers. Steve Jobs theorized that his cancer might have come from his habit of sitting his laptop directly on his lap and working on it for hours at a time. There is a small but growing suspicion that the giant batteries used in electric cars, particularly Teslas, cause cancer. They are toxic waste when dead. Lithium batteries, even for toys, carry a warning about careful, separate disposal. And let's remember: the tobacco industry vehemently insisted that smoking tobacco did not cause cancer. Medical doctors appeared in ads for cigarettes. Nothing to worry about here, right?

Everywhere they can take land in rural areas and small towns, adjacent to housing developments, schools, hospitals the A.I. industry is building data centers the size of multiple aircraft carriers supposedly to have their own nuclear reactors and electricity production plants running electricity through, above, under and all around their 'campuses.' What is a safe radius of empty land around one of these? Nobody knows. Nobody cares. Yet. The oceans of water the facility uses to cool its chips and reactors has to be dumped. Is it toxic? Nobody knows. Nobody cares. Yet.

Maybe this is the means being used by already landed aliens walking amongst us, to colonize earth as their factory with all of us enslaved workers (like China has). Look at Gates' face, Musk's face, Zuckerberg's face and tell me they don't look like aliens. Or maybe this can also so clutter space that A.I. factories are crashing into each other and falling to earth as debris as big as asteroids, destroying cities, throwing Earth out of orbit so we all cook or freeze. These A.I.

promoters have also been climate change hucksters telling us we'll soon all be under water (while they buy $10-million beachfront homes). Not to be trusted. All this so your kid doesn't have to write his own term paper and can have an A.I. fake friend, like the evil witch's magic mirror that, whenever asked "who's the fairest of them all?" answered "You are, my Queen."

I think all of you being stampeded into embracing ChatGPT, Claude, Gemini, and all the rest of it are fools, making yourself and those you influence irrelevant. If I accept what A.I. will tell me as gospel, I no longer need my CPA, lawyer, financial advisor, doctor, shrink, or even my spouse. And your clients or employers won't need you either. Too many of my clients ARE embracing and using various A.I. applications as fast as they can, and it makes me sad for them. The world will fast refuse to pay them for their expertise, experience, education, etc. and turn to "all know-how needed must be free" by asking ChatGPT for a summary. They are like the kindly person who finds the orphaned baby bear, parents killed. She takes the bear in and is delighted to discover it acts like a dog, eating when served, learning tricks, fully domesticated. Until one morning, the now grown bear decides enough of this pandering to this silly old woman and it grabs her, tears her into bite-sized pieces and eats her. As you "convert" your business and YOUR key contributions to it to 'done by A.I.', you think you have a domesticated bear. A willing pet. Just wait.

At Least Hedge Your Bets

*(As An Investor
AND With Your Own Business)*

In my youth, one of the guys I recruited in my Amway downline was a White Castle short order cook managing to be a very successful ladies' man. He resembled Elvis including the big sideburns, dressed for disco, and drove a purple Dodge Challenger with white interior. He had seven girlfriends, to hedge his bets and prevent even one night without companionship. He also recruited all seven and had them focused on retailing cosmetics – so they all knew he was in Amway. They did not know there were seven. Each thought there was but one. (Note for marketing: people believe what they want to believe.) So, when they all decided, each independently, to surprise him and show up at a big Amway convention, they all surprised each other, too. Even though I was watching money evaporate before my eyes, the entertainment was worth it. It got loud, physical, very Ladies of WWE. Hedging bets is smart, but not that way.

So, Is A.I. MANIA a Tulip Mania, anotherDot.Com Bubble, another NFT scam? Or real? The next gold rush where everyone in early gets richer than rich? If you're invested as I am, heavy in tech, in A.I.-tied companies, you might want to hedge your bets (which IS what they are) with some cash held as cash (Buffett is at 22% T-Bills 3/26) and some dull, ordinary companies that make stuff people need, want and buy. Like, for example, home builders because we have a monstrous inventory shortage and a political interest by Trump and by Democrats in meddling in this market. I already owned a few homebuilder stocks. After listening to Meredith Whitney on the subject in February, 2026 I added her recommended one. (NOT intended as investing advice. Here for example purposes only.) A multi-split-test in direct marketing i.e. 6 lists, not 1 or 2 against 2 or 3 headlines and themes, not 1, etc. is the way smart direct marketers and copywriters hedge their bets. A fake psychic does it with cold reads and both sides statements like "I can sense that some people think of you as selfish even though you have often sacrificed for others your whole life. You are of generous spirit but also a somewhat private person who tends not to advertise her generosity." Make a note, by the way: people LOVE "being read," being told things about themselves. **Every day with your business, you bet on things, on people, on ideas – but do you hedge? A lot don't. They fall victim to being all in on a "one," the worst number in business.** There's a TV ad for Spectrum, with a boutique hotel owner praising Spectrum, saying "we are totally dependent on them for internet, for entertainment for our guests, for Wi-Fi...we couldn't even check a guest in or out without them." I want to scream when I watch it. I always had more than one credit card merchant account and divided business between them, keeping them all active (their contracts be damned). I sure as hell wouldn't be unable to operate my hotel if Spectrum went down for a day or a week. Years ago, I was working a Gary Halbert seminar in Key West, Florida when a hurricane came roaring toward us, the island locked down, with no electricity. I was astounded that a big, pricey hotel in Key West wouldn't have a back-up generator. We couldn't cook food, light rooms, get air conditioning but fortunately no power was needed to access the booze, the grand piano and non-refrigerated food so we survived two days in this dire situation. You could look out through the glass walls by the piano and see the alligators swimming by. The hotel staff abandoned ship and left the entire place to us at the start of the flooding. I was rooting for the gators' – my thought was: if you're on hurricane island without a generator, you deserve to be eaten.

Sorry to say it, but there are a lot of business owners who deserve to fail, a lot of people who deserve to be broke because they are out there with no back-up plan, no back-up cash reserves or credit, no hedging of their bets. During the funding fight amongst reprehensible politicians, the TSA went unfunded for weeks with TSA agents forced by law to work without pay. Obviously, this is unfair. And yes, their salary is not very high; starting around $50,000.00, and many live in expensive major cities. But all that said, the fact that they couldn't go without two paychecks without being broke, needing free food from food banks set up at airports just for them, couldn't afford gas to get to work Is ridiculous. I was once that broke, but I was not drawing regular paychecks at all, not making $50,000.00 a year. My cash reserves were coins in the couch cushions. I had no Plan B because I didn't even have a Plan A. But as soon as I fixed all that, I started to create reserves and always built a B if starting an A.

A.I. is seducing investors to way, way over-weight their portfolios to tech companies themselves making huge investments in A.I. and claiming some A,I. advantage. Some are so over-weighted that if (when?) a hurricane comes to A.I., they'll have no back-up generator.

A.I. is seducing business owners to "drop everything" and join the mad rush to catch up with A.I.'ing every aspect of their business. This is a MAD rush indeed.

INVESTORS: What to do? Slow down. Investors do just fine coming in gradually, carefully, slowly to a new golden opportunity. You do NOT have to be first. Usually letting a new category of business opportunity and activity get sorted out a little is better for investors than being there on its Day One. I have made millions from buying stock in Apple, Amazon, Microsoft, starting quite late, only after my own determination of what these companies were and would be going forward said to buy, now.

BUSINESS OWNERS: What to do? Slow down. NEVER unplug anything to plug in something new until you have separately tested the new. Be wary of consolidating many functions of your business or your advertising and marketing into one software, technology, or A.I. driven system without a back-up generator. Be alert for irrational exuberance, yours or staff's, causing you to stop doing what works and is profitable to re-allocate resources to one new thing.

It is so common it's a cliché: long-married man hits it big financially or for other reasons is seduced away from that wife to "run away" with a new one half his age. Watch the movie 'Network' with Bill Holden and Faye Dunaway. Or check the end years of Frank Sinatra's and Dean Martin's lives. Read up. More often than not, the pairing of Mr. Older & Set In His Ways with the New, Younger, Exciting But Exhausting Model fails. Humbled, tired and sorry, he comes back home to Original Wife. **I have watched this very same show often with business owners.** I see them lose interest in what is working reliably and consistently in their business and ultimately leave it to turn all attention to something new, exciting, magical, easier, cheaper; something the cool kids (peers) are all doing. A.I. is especially magical. But these are going to be a whale of a lot of business owners having to play Bill Holden's role and come home to what works. I don't want you to be that guy.

When Henry Ford started selling the Model T, it was exciting, people wanted to be the first in their neighborhood to have one, but the motorcar was quickly, infamously unreliable. Ford never ran it, but an ad man of the era, whose name I can't recall, wrote an ad for the car with a picture of a farmer and his wife next to their new car, with the headline: "BE A PROUD OWNER OF THE MODEL-T MOTORCAR – BUT DO KEEP A HORSE IN THE BARN."

The Great Tulip Mania

The Dutch Republic and Holland were among the richest nations in the world in the 1600s to the 1700s. It was the Dutch Gilded Age. Tulips were introduced in 1637, and almost instantly, speculative investing in tulip bulbs and tulip "futures" began. The price of a tulip future reached a peak price equal to that of a big mansion on the Amsterdam Grand Canal. In short order, everybody was obsessed with investing in tulips. People went into debt to do so. People were investing ten times their annual incomes. Auctions were held in taverns. TULIP MANIA reached its peak in the winter of 1636 – 1637, when some tulip contracts were changing hands five times. Most contracts were never filled, and in February, 1637, prices collapsed and trading stopped.

For a more complete report, check TULIP MANIA at Wikipedia.

Today, TULIP MANIA is the metaphor used for all financial manias, when investing is replaced with wild speculation and prices are not linked to inherent, intrinsic or predictable values. Sound familiar?

AUTHOR'S AFTERWORD

"If man was meant to fly, God would have given us wings."

OK. I get it. ALL cautions against progress and against new technology are discarded in the same wastebasket.

I'll quote the great American philosopher Bill Maher: "Be more skeptical."

People infected with Greenspan's irrational exuberance may ignite the making of all the money, but skeptics wind up keeping most of it. A person with a really great mind can be both optimist and pessimist, eager earliest adopter and skeptic....operating somewhere in the middle.

I put EMERGENCY in this book's title because my skeptic side sees one in the wild lust and nearly thoughtless embrace of A.I. Too much is being embraced too fast because nobody wants to be called slow. I've created and teach an entire Course in 'Mind Hijacking', I know exactly how it's done, and can see it in all its glory with the A.I. Revolution.

To be clear, I'm not suggesting you sit this one out. I've included a lot of strategy for participating. But at the same time, it is possible to be analytical, critical, questioning. I've raised many points for that. I hope 'n pray you did not have your A.I. read this book for you and summarize it for you – by its own bias, its own agenda, it might well have omitted something important but skeptical and therefore unwelcome.

ABOUT THE AUTHOR

DAN S. KENNEDY is the provocative, truth-telling author of the popular "NO B.S." book series and regular contributor to a number of newsletters, including The No B.S. Magnetic Marketing Letter. He is a multi-millionaire, serial entrepreneur and a trusted advisor, strategy consultant and ad copywriter for hundreds of small to mid-sized businesses, although some have grown to valuations and/or been sold for $50-Million to $1-Billion. His methods have made successes in over 200 different industries and professions. As a speaker, he has repeatedly appeared on programs with celebrity entrepreneurs like Kathy Ireland, Debbi Fields, George Foreman and Gene Simmons; with top business speakers like Brian Tracy, Zig Ziglar, Tom Hopkins and Jim Rohn; four former Presidents, Gen. Schwarzkopf, Secretary Colin Powell and Lady Margaret Thatcher....addressing audiences from

500 to 35,000 including 9 years on the largest public seminar tour of all time.

Other Books by Dan Kennedy

No B.S. Guides to....
Selling Your Company for Top Dollar
Successful Marketing Automation
Time Management for Entrepreneurs (4th Edition)
Direct Marketing for NON-Direct Marketing Businesses (4th Edition)
Succeeding In Business by Breaking ALL The Rules
Ruthless Management of People and Profits
Marketing to the Affluent (4th Edition)

These and other No B.S. books are available at Amazon. Audio Books at Audible.com.

Additional Dan Kennedy Resources at Magnetic-Marketing.com. And his private Dan Kennedy Letter at Pete Lillo Publishing, Phone/Fax 330-922-9833.

www.ingramcontent.com/pod-product-compliance
Lightning Source LLC
Chambersburg PA
CBHW040517220526
45473CB00012B/2893